SHORT CIRCULAR

LAKE DISTRICT

by

JOHN N. MERRILL

Maps and photographs by John N. Merrill

TRAIL CREST PUBLICATIONS Ltd.,
- *"from footprint to finished book."*

1993

Sandia Mountains
New Mexico. USA

TRAIL CREST PUBLICATIONS Ltd.,
WINSTER, MATLOCK, DERBYSHIRE. DE4 2DQ
☎ (0629) 826354
FAX (0629) 826354

Edited, typeset, designed, paged, printed, marketed and distributed by John N. Merrill.

First Published - August 1993

ISBN 1 874754 20 9

U.S.A. office - P.O.Box 124. Santa Rosa, New Mexico. 88435 U.S.A.

Please note - The maps in this guide are purely illustrative. You are encouraged to use the appropriate 1:25,000 O.S. map.
Meticulous research has been undertaken to ensure that this publication is highly accurate at the time of going to press. The publishers, however, cannot be held responsible for alterations, errors or omissions, but they would welcome notification of such for future editions.

Typeset in - Bookman - bold, italic and plain 9pt and 18pt.

Printed by - John N. Merrill at Milne House, Speedwell Mill, Miller's Green, Wirksworth, Derbyshire. DE4 4BL
Cover sketch - "Lakeland sunset." © Suncrest Ventures Ltd.

An all British product.

ABOUT JOHN N. MERRILL

Born in the flatlands of Bedfordshire he soon moved to Sheffield and discovered the joy of the countryside in the Peak District, where he lives. A keen walker who travels the world exploring mountains and trails. Over the last twenty years he has walked more than 150,000 miles - including the first walk around the entire coastline of Britain, 7,000 miles - and worn out over sixty pairs of boots. He has written more than 120 walk guides to areas in Britain and abroad, and created numerous challenge walks which have been used to raise more than £500,000 for charity. New Mexico, USA is his second home.

CONTENTS

INTRODUCTION

The walks selected in this guide stem from my many visits to the Lakes. First from school days leading a party, onto a month at the Eskdale Mountain School - for training!, a circular walk taking in all the major summits, and numerous week-end forays - winter and summer. Selecting fifteen walks for my first guide, was hard. Having made my selection I had to stick rigidly to my plan as other places looked so fascinating. The scope is endless but I wanted to show the variety of walking, while combining it with my favourite areas. In the end I did all the walks in six days, starting in fine weather and ending up in the pouring rain!

Some are short, some long, some easy, some hard, but combined they illustrate the huge variety of walking in the Lakes, from gentle strolls around a lake to walking along an exposed ridge. The Grasmere/Rydal Water walk I wrote about twenty years ago. Yewbarrow above Wastwater still remains one of my favourite mountains, with a scramble up and down. The ridge of Hopegill Head near Crummock Water, is of high quality, while the views from the ridge of Illgill Head above Wastwater are matchless. The walk around Ullswater and onto the summit of Place Fell, is among the finest anywhere. Hellvellyn, one of the Lakeland *"Munro's"*, has always been a firm favourite, and I have now stood on its summit more than forty times, and still enjoy it! In south Lakeland are gentler walks with extensive views, from Hawkshead and in Grizedale Forest. While, as a parting shot, the walk around Kentmere is extremely beautiful and quiet. These then are some of my favourite walks and hope you enjoy them as much as I.

Happy walking!

John N. Merrill

ABOUT THE WALKS

Whilst every care is taken detailing and describing the walk in this book, it should be borne in mind that the countryside changes by the seasons and the work of man. I have described the walk to the best of my ability, detailing what I have found on the walk in the way of stiles and signs. Obviously with the passage of time stiles become broken or replaced by a ladder stile or even a small gate. Signs too have a habit of being broken or pushed over. All the route follow rights of way and only on rare occasions will you have to overcome obstacles in its path, such as a barbed wire fence or electric fence. On rare occasions rights of way are rerouted and these ammendments are included in the next edition.

The seasons bring occasional problems whilst out walking which should also be borne in mind. In the height of summer paths become overgrown and you will have to fight your way through in a few places. In low lying areas the fields are often full of crops, and although the pathline goes straight across it may be more practical to walk round the field edge to get to the next stile or gate. In summer the ground is generally dry but in autumn and winter, especially because of our climate, the surface can be decidedly wet and slippery; sometimes even gluttonous mud!

These comments are part of countryside walking which help to make your walk more interesting or briefly frustrating. Standing in a farmyard up to your ankles in mud might not be funny at the time but upon reflection was one of the highlights of the walk!

The mileage for each walk is based on three calculations -

1. pedometer reading.
2. the route map measured on the map.
3. the time I took for the walk.

I believe the figure stated for each walk to be very accurate but we all walk differently and not always in a straight line! The time allowed for each walk is on the generous side and does not include pub stops etc. The figure is based on the fact that on average a person walks 2 1/2 miles an hours but less in hilly terrain.

Thirlmere, from the western slopes of Helvellyn.

24 Hour Lake District Weather Forecast

☎ 05394 - 45151

Information Centres -

Bowness Bay - ☎ 05394 42895

Coniston - ☎ 05394 - 41533

Grasmere - ☎ 05394 - 35245

Hawkshead - ☎ 05394 - 36525

Keswick - ☎ 07687 - 72803

Pooley Bridge - ☎ 07684 - 86530

Seatoller - ☎ 07687 - 77294

Ullswater - ☎ 07684 - 82414

Waterhead - ☎ 05394 - 32729

GRASMERE AND RYDAL WATER - 6 MILES

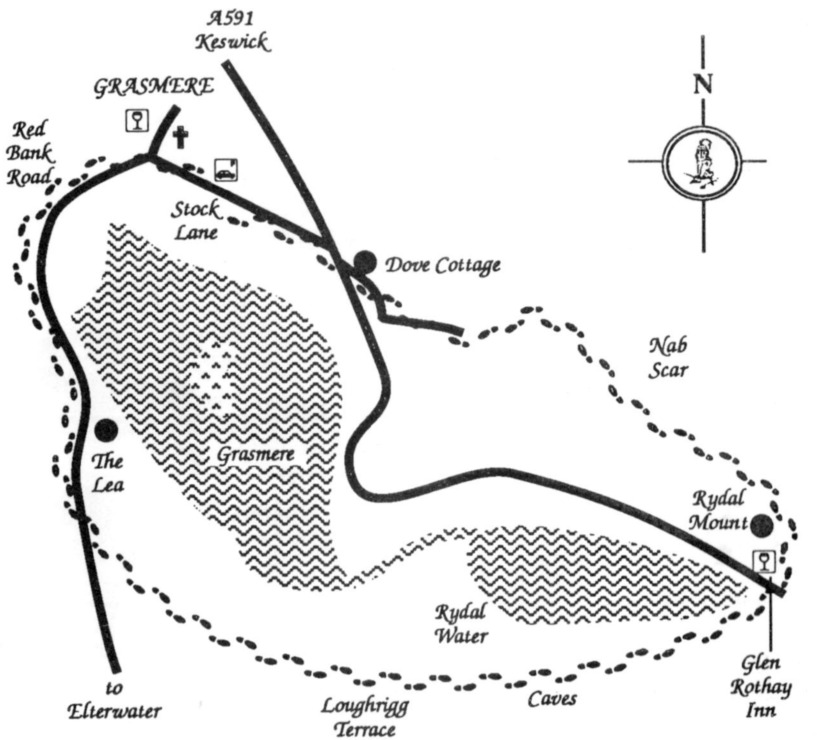

Rydal Water.

GRASMERE AND RYDAL WATER - 6 MILES

- a Wordsworth walk.

- allow 2 1/2 hours.

- Grasmere - The Lea - Redbank Wood - Loughrigg Terrace - Jobson Close - Steps End - Rydal - Rydal Mount - How Top - Dove Cottage - Grasmere.

1:25,000 Outdoor Leisure Map - No. 7 - The English Lakes - South Eastern area.

- Stock Lane, Grasmere.

Several in Grasmere. Glen Rothay Inn, Rydal.

- Several in Grasmere.

ABOUT THE WALK - Stunning! I first wrote about this circuit 20 years ago and still enjoy walking it. The walk is surrounded by beautiful scenery with high fells set against the lakes - Grasmere and Rydal Water. It is a scene loved by William Wordsworth and as you walk round you can see his grave, and his former homes - Rydal Mount and Dove Cottage - both are open to the public. Grasmere is an attractive village and well worth exploring, while here. The walk is done anti-clockwise.

WALKING INSTRUCTIONS - From the car park on Stock Lane, turn right into Grasmere and opposite the church turn left along Red Bank Road. Keep on the road for 3/4 mile to the house, The Lea. Here bear right on a No Through Road, footpath sign - *"Langdale"*, and a track. Gently ascend for 1/4 mile to a metal seat and kissing gate. Go through the gate and follow the path through Redbank Wood to Red Bank Road, reached via a kissing gate, little over 1/4 mile away. Turn right and in a few yards left along a track to another kissing gate. Continue ahead on a path around *"Loughrigg Terrace"* - exceptionally beautiful in Spring when the bluebells are out. Reach a seat on the "ridge" in less 1/2 mile and continue on the path contouring round the fell side to some old quarries with impressive cave, 1/2 mile away. Just after enter woodland and descend towards Rydal Water. Gaining another path, turn left then right to a kissing gate and enter Rydal Woods. Follow the path to another kissing gate and onto a footbridge and the A591 road at Rydal.

Turn right, passing Glen Rothay Inn and in a few yards turn left, passing St. Mary's church and on past the entrance to Rydal Mount. Just after turn left along the bridlepath - *"Grasmere."* The track is well gated and contours round the fell, through woodland and across fields and in 1 1/2 miles becomes tarmaced. Keep right at a small pond and in 1/4 mile reach How Top. Continue descending the lane past Dove Cottage to the A591 road. Turn right then left and walk along Stock Lane back to your start.

William Wordsworth (1770 - 1850) - Lakelands' best loved poet. He lived at Dove Cottage 1799 - 1808 and Rydal Mount from 1813 to his death in 1850. In 1843 he was appointed Poet Laureate. In 1835 his book - *"Guide through the District of the Lakes"*, was published.

Grasmere.

REMEMBER AND OBSERVE THE COUNTRY CODE

Enjoy the countryside and respect its life and work.

Guard against all risk of fire.

Fasten all gates.

Keep your dogs under close control.

Keep to public paths across farmland.

Use gates and stiles to cross fences, hedges and walls.

Leave livestock, crops and machinery alone.

Take your litter home - pack it in; pack it out.

Help to keep all water clean.

Protect wildlife, plants and trees.

Take special care on country roads

Make no unnecessary noise.

KENTMERE - 6 1/2 MILES

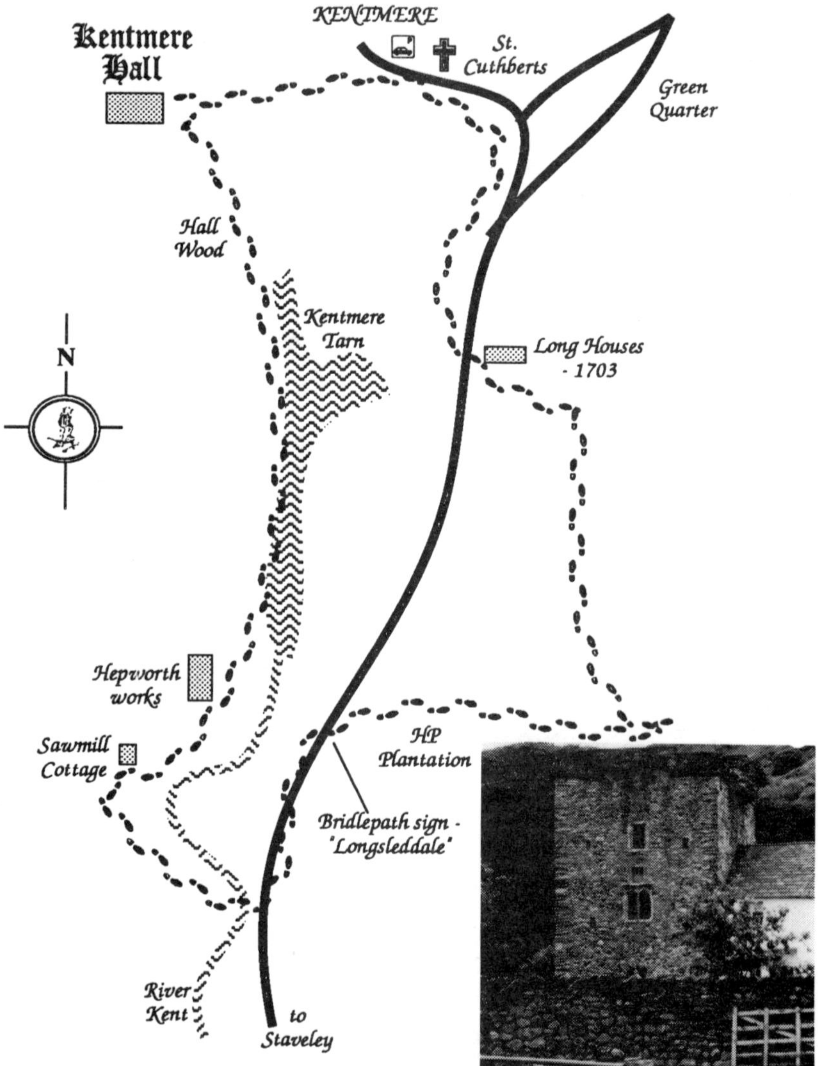

KENTMERE HALL - In 1517 Bernard Gilpin was born here. He became the Arch-deacon of Durham, earning himself the title of the "Apostle of the North." Legends surround the hall and one states that the Troutbeck giant - Hugh Hird - walked past when the hall was being built. Several men were struggling to lift a large beam into place in the kitchen. Hugh picked up the 30 foot long, 13 inches wide by 12 inches tall, beam alone and placed it into position.

KENTMERE - 6 1/2 MILES

- allow 2 1/2 hours.

Kentmere - Kentmere Hall - Hall Wood - Kentmere Tarn - Sawmill Cottage - Ullthwaite Bridge - HP Plantation - Nuttera Beck - Long Houses - Kentmere.

1:25,000 Outdoor Leisure Map No.7 - The English Lakes - South Eastern area.

Limited parking near church in Kentmere.

- Nothing!

ABOUT THE WALK - A delightful walk in a quiet and peaceful area of southern Lakeland.

WALKING INSTRUCTIONS - From the car park, walk past the church, dedicated to St. Cuthbert, and turn right along the drive, bridlepath sign - *"Kentmere Hall."* Approaching the hall turn left to a gate. Follow a grass track to a gate and Hall Wood. Walk beside it for a short distance before entering it. Where the track forks keep to the lefthand one and soon reach another gate at the end of the wood. Continue on the well defined path/track with Kentmere Tarn on your left - full of waterfowl and mute swans with their cygnets. Continue on the path for 3/4 mile to the Hepworth Minerals and Chemical works. Walk through the works and bear right along the tarmaced drive to Sawmill Cottage (pottery). Here turn left at the entrance and follow the path to a footbridge over the River Kent. Continue along the walled path to a T junction and turn left. Follow the walled track to Ullthwaite Bridge and road to Kentmere. Turn left along the road for nearly 1/4 mile to a gate and footpath sign - *"Longsleddale"* - on your right. Turn right and walk around the edge of HP Plantation to a gate - following a track. Continue ascending gently leaving the plantation and in 1/4 reach a path junction, close to a wall. Turn left (northwards), following a faint path across the field to a gate. Continue to another and keep to the lefthand edge of the field to another gate, just after Nuttera Beck. Here turn left and follow a track as you descend to a stile. Continue on to more gates and houses dated 1703 - Long Houses. Just after gain the Kentmere road and turn right. In 1/4 mile turn left and follow the lane back to Kentmere church.

AMBLESIDE AND TROUTBECK - 8 MILES

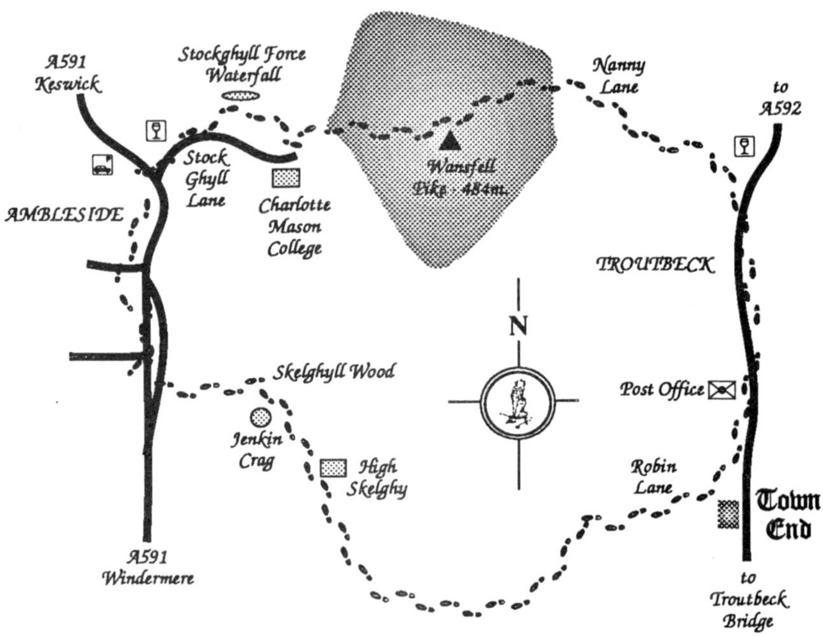

From opposite page - Windermere from here - and onto a bridge over Stencher Beck. Continue ahead on the track following it round and down to Ambleside. Instead of turning right and following the main road , follow the road just before it back into central Ambleside and retrace your steps back to the car park.

BRIDGE HOUSE, AMBLESIDE - Bought by the National Trust in 1928. In the 18th century it was a summer house for Amblesdie Hall.

TOWN END, TROUTBECK - A yoeman's farmer's house built in 1626.

AMBLESIDE AND TROUTBECK - 8 MILES

- allow 3 hours.

Ambleside - Stockghyll Force - Wansfell Pike (484m.) - Nanny Lane - Troutbeck - Robin Lane - Jenkin Crag - Skelghyll Wood - Ambleside.

O.S. MAP ***1:25,000 Outdoor Leisure map No. 7 - The English Lakes - South Eastern area.***

P - ***Ambleside.***

- ***Numerous in Ambleside. Hotel in Troutbeck.***

ABOUT THE WALK - Delightful low lying country with magnificent views over Windermere from Wansfell Pike and Jenkin Crag. Near the start you walk past Stockghyll Force and in Troutbeck you can extend the walk by 1/2 mile to visit the National Trust property - Town End.

WALKING INSTRUCTIONS - From Ambleside's main car park, return to the road and turn right past past the National Trust Bridge House and after the Salutation Hotel, turn left along the lane - Stockghyll Lane - to Stockghyll Force. Walk into the Country Park and ascend to the force and turn right to a kissing gate. Through this with Charlotte Mason College on your right, turn left to a cattle grid and road to Grove Farm. In a few yards turn right at a ladder stile and footpath sign - *"Troutbeck via Wansfell."* Begin ascending and soon reach another ladder stile. Continue ascending on a distinct path for 1/2 mile to the summit of Wansfell Pike, 484m. Continue to a ladder stile and path sign - *"Troutbeck via Nanny Lane - follow cairns."* Start descending the defined path and in 1/2 mile reach a gate. 80 yards later reach another and Nanny Lane. Turn right and descend the walled track to the road in Troutbeck. Turn right and walk along the road to the Post Office and shop 1/2 mile away. En route notice the wells in the wall on your right - St. Margaret, St. James, St. John. Just past the Post Office turn right, as bridlepath signed - *"Ambleside"* and follow Robin Lane, a track. (If you continue down the road a short distance you come to Town End.) Follow the track for 1/2 mile to a kissing gate and Ambleside sign. Keep left on the path to another kissing gate and onto the tarmaced lane at High Skelghyll. Continue to a gate and another and follow a track into Skelghyll Wood and Jenkin Crag, National Trust property. Follow the track past the crag on your left - great views of

HAWKSHEAD AND LATTERBARROW - 6 MILES

Latterbarrow Cairn.

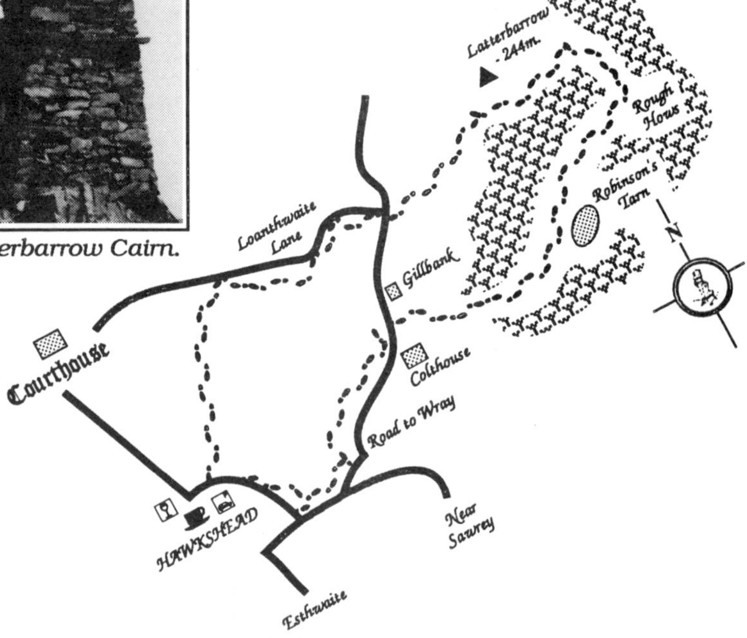

Hawkshead.

HAWKSHEAD AND LATTERBARROW - 6 MILES

- allow 2 1/2 hours.

Hawkshead - Gillbank - Rough Hows - Old Intake - Latterbarrow - Loanthwaite Lane - Hawkshead.

1:25,000 Outdoor Leisure Map No. 7 - The English Lakes - South Eastern area.

- Hawkshead

- Several in Hawkshead.

ABOUT THE WALK - Hawkshead is Beatrice Potter country and a very popular village, full of quaint houses. This walk leads you into the surrounding countryside, through forest to the summit of Latterbarrow for an unparalleled view. You return through woodland and across fields to Hawkshead.

WALKING INSTRUCTIONS - From the car park return to the road - North Lonsdale Road - and turn right. At the end turn left and just after the bridge left again along the road to Wray. 1/3 mile along here before Gillbank, turn right at a gate and bridlepath sign - *"Claife Heights."* Follow the track through Colthouse Plantation, gently ascending and in more than 1/4 mile reach a gate. Continue onto another in 1/4 mile and on your right is a small tarn, which in July is covered with lilies, and in the surrounding area spotted heath orchids grow. Continue on the forest track to another gate in Rough Hows. 1/4 mile later turn left, as footpath signed - *Latterbarrow.* The path keeps near a wall on your right and curves round to your left, guided by white topped posts. In 1/2 mile cross a footbridge and 100 yards later turn right at a stile and ascend in open country to the tall cairn on the summit of Latterbarrow. Turn left and descend the defined path to a track and continue down it to a gate and lane. Turn left then right along Loanthwaite Lane. Walk along this for a 1/3 mile to a gate and footpath sign - *"Hawkshead."* Keep the hedge on your left to a track - Scar House Lane. Turn left along it for a few yards before turning right at a kissing gate and guided by these reach Hawkshead. Cross the road and walk past the houses into the centre and turn left. Along here you come to the car park where you began.

GRIZEDALE FOREST & SATTERTHWAITE - 8 MILES

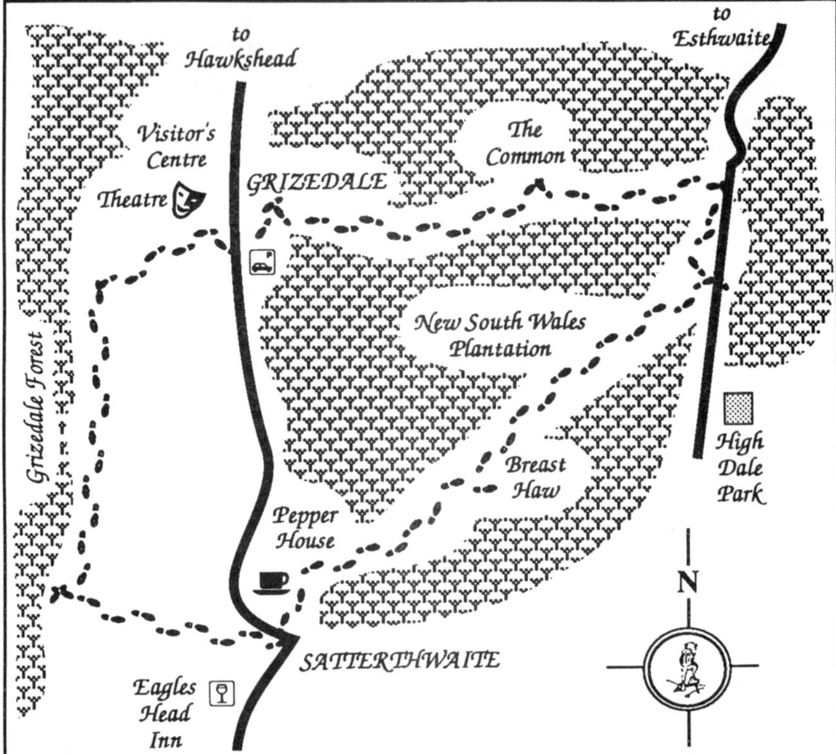

Eagles Head Inn, Satterthwaite.

GRIZEDALE FOREST & SATTERTHWAITE - 8 MILES

- allow 3 hours.

- Grizedale - Grizedale Forest - Satterthwaite - Breast Haw - New South Wales Plantation - Low Scar Wood - The Cross - The Common - Potato Peg Plantation - Grizedale.

O.S. MAP ***1:25,000 Outdoor Leisure Map No. 7 - The English Lakes - South Eastern area.***

P ***- Grizedale***

- Eagles Head, Satterthwaite.

Grizedale. Pepper House, Satterthwaite.

ABOUT THE WALK - A beautiful walk in the forest with a pub halfway! It is all on well defined paths and tracks and is walked anti-clockwise.

WALKING INSTRUCTIONS - From the car park return to the main road and walk down the lefthand side of of Grizedale Forest Museum complex and Theatre. Keep left on a track before the forest, following a cycle route. The track ascends a field and in 1/4 mile enters the forest and you keep just inside the forest for the next mile. Here turn left on a track to a gate and open country. Follow the track to the road at Satterthwaite, 1/2 mile away. Turn right then left past Pepper House and follow the lane around to your left. (If you keep right along the road in Satterthwaite, just past the church is the Eagles Head Inn.) Before the house on the lane turn right, as bridlepath signed - *"Dale Park."* The track/path is well defined and you will cross several forest roads not marked on the map. Basically you keep straight ahead for 1 1/4 miles through the forest, past Breast Haw, New South Wales Plantation, before dropping down to the minor road from Esthwaite. Turn left along the road and 1/4 mile later, left again, as bridlepath signed, and follow a track. The path/track zig-zags around and in 1/2 mile reaches a forest road. Cross to a gate and continue on the defined path, and in 1/4 mile pass a prominent metal chimney on your right. Keep a wall on your right and reach a gate. Cross another forest track and continue on a track to another. Cross over and continue on the track which soon hugs the perimeter of the forest as it descends back to Grizedale.

CRINKLE CRAGS & PIKE OF BLISCO - 5 MILES

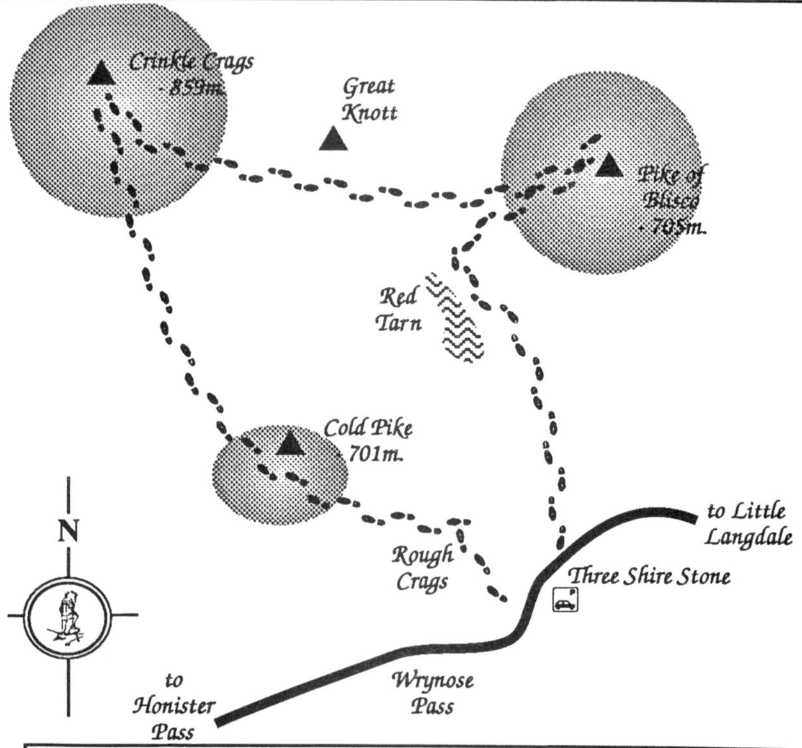

View to Pike of Blisco and Red Tarn.

CRINKLE CRAGS & PIKE OF BLISCO - 5 MILES

- allow 3 hours.

- Three Shire Stone, Wrynose Pass - Cold Pike - Crinkle Crags - Great Knott - Red Tarn - Pike of Blisco - Three Shire Stone.

1:25,000 Outdoor Leisure Map No. 6 - The English Lakes - South Western area.

Limited parking on the summit of Wyrnose Pass, near Three Shire Stone. Grid Ref.277027.

ABOUT THE WALK - The Wyrnose Pass climbs through majestic scenery and from its summit, several peaks are within easy reach. The route takes you to two of them - Crinkle Crags and Pike of Blisco and involves some 800 metres of ascent. For a shorter ascent you can just climb one or the other. Crinkle Crags is a magnificent view point to the Scafell area, whereas, Pike of Blisco is a stunning gallery for the Langdale Pikes and valley. Choose a fine day for the walk for in bad weather it can be a wild and unforgiving. No inns on this walk!

WALKING INSTRUCTIONS - From Three Shire Stone, head north west, following the lefthand path across the infant River Duddon and ascend Rough Crags to Cold Pike (701m.) Descend slightly before ascending to the summit of Crinkle Crags (859m.), 1 1/2 miles away. The ascent in the final stages is quite steep. Return to the base of the crags and bear left following the path over Great Knott to Red Tarn. Here the final 200 metre ascent begins to the summit of Pike of Blisco. Return to Red Tarn and turn left following the wide path down to Three Shire Stone.

Path up Pike of Blisco from near Red Tarn.

YEWBARROW - 628m, - 5 MILES

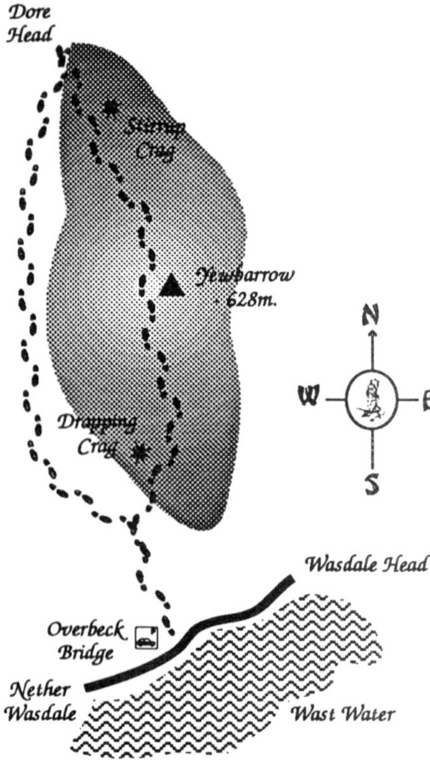

Stirrup Crag.

Dropping Crag (Overbeck).

YEWBARROW
- 628m.
- 5 MILES
- allow 2 hours.

Overbeck Bridge - Dropping Crag - Great Door - Yewbarrow - Stirrup Crag - Dore Head - Dropping Crag - Overbeck Bridge.

O.S. MAP ***1:25,000 Outdoor leisure map - No. 6 - The English Lakes - South Western area.***

P ***- Overbeck Bridge. Grid Ref: 168068.***

None - nearest at Wasdale Head, 2 1/2 miles away.

ABOUT THE WALK - A fine mountain at the entrance to Wasdale. Some of my earliest rock climbs were on Dropping Crag (Overbeck), and as a result the mountain remains a firm favourite. The walk is a short one but involves a little rock scrambling up and down, but the views are stunning. 600 metres of ascent.

WALKING INSTRUCTIONS. Walk out of the top righthand corner of the car park with Overbeck (stream) on your left. Reach a kissing gate and turn right and begin ascending the prominent shoulder close to a fence, towards Dropping Crag. Go over a ladder stile and continue ascending on the right of the crag. You will have to a little rock scrambling as you ascend through Great Door. Continue on the path along the ridge to the summit of Yewbarrow. Continue beyond, traversing the mountain and in 1/2 mile reach the top of Stirrup Crag. Descend on the path, steeply, and sometimes scrambling to the Dore Head. Turn left and descend the gentle path which soon contours round to your left, around the slopes of Yewbarrow. 1 1/2 miles from Dore Head regain you earlier path near Dropping Crag and descend back to the car park.

LLIGILL HEAD & THE SCREES, WAST WATER - 10 MILES

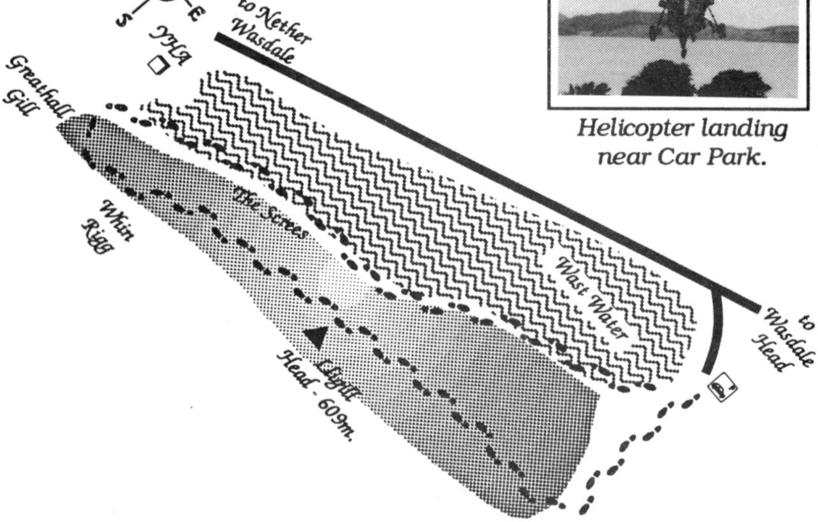

Helicopter landing near Car Park.

Wast Water from near Greathall Gill.

LLIGILL HEAD & THE SCREES, WAST WATER - 10 MILES

- allow 4 hours

- National Trust Car Park - Lligill Head, 603m. - Whin Rigg - Greathall Gill - The Screes - Lakeshore path - Wast Water - National Trust Car Park.

1:25,000 Outdoor Leisure Map No. 6 - The English Lakes - South Western area.

National Trust at northern end of Wast Water. Grid Ref. 184075.

- None. Nearest little over a mile away at Wasdale Head.

ABOUT THE WALK - The longest walk in the book, but one of the finest! I have long regarded the ridge from Lligill Head to Whin Rigg, one of the best ridge walks in the Lake District. The views are stunning to the sea, while behind the might of Scafell and Great Gable provide an amazing contrast. You traverse the mountain and return along the shore of Wast Water. The path in the southern end is quite rugged and includes 1/2 mile of boulder hopping across The Screes. I spent a month at the Eskdale Mountain School and it was in this area that I became "initiated!"

WALKING INSTRUCTIONS - Gain the track from the car park and turn left along it. In a short distance is the *"Lakeshore"* path sign on your right - this is your return walk. Continue ahead and soon ascend through Fence Wood and onto the fell. In a mile from the car park, turn right and ascend the slopes of Lligill Head - there are two paths, one soon after the trees and another 1/4 mile later. Both join up. In more than a mile reach the trig point 603m. of Lligill Head. For the next two miles walk along the broad ridge with crags and screes of Wast Water on your right. Ascend over Whin Rigg, 535m. and 1/2 mile later before reaching the prominent wide gully of Greathall Gill, turn right at a cairn and descend the small path, steeply to a stile at the base of the fell. Cross this and continue to another and turn right to a kissing gate. Here pick up the Lakeshore path and begin the 4 mile walk close to Wast Water back to the car park. The path is defined but after 1/2 mile you cross a large scree slope. Look for cairns as you cross. With this behind you, you are on easier ground and in an hour you are back at your starting out path. Turn left back to the car park.

HELVELLYN - 950m. - 8 MILES

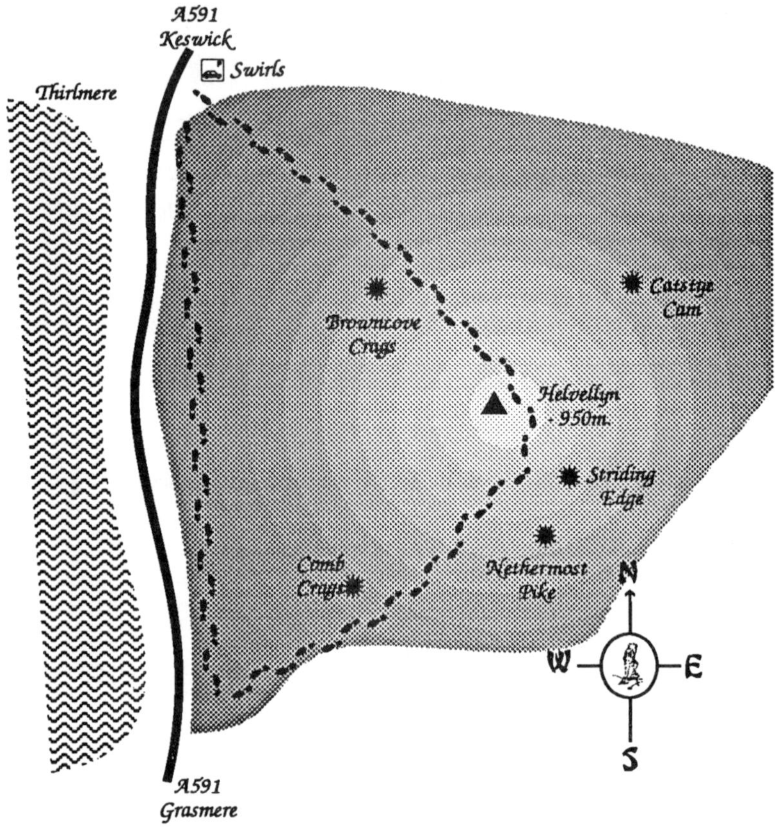

Striding Edge, Helvellyn.

HELVELLYN
- 950m.
- 8 MILES
- allow 4 hours.

- Swirls Car Park - Browncove Crags - Lower Man - Helvellyn - Birk Side - Swirls Forest - Swirls Car Park.

O.S. MAP ***1:25,000 Outdoor Leisure Map No.5 - The English Lakes - North East Sheet.***

Just off the A591 road - Swirls Car Park - Grid Ref. 317169.

Nothing - carry what you need. Nearest 1/2 mile along the A591 road at Thirlspot.

ABOUT THE WALK - Still remains one of the finest mountain ascents in England. Although one of the longest walks in the book with 1,000 metres of ascent, the effort is worth it to stand on the top of one of the Lakeland Munroe's. The views are extensive, especially to Catstye Cam, Red Tarn, and ofcourse, Striding Edge. You traverse the mountain and return through quiet forest, where I have often seen deer. A walk to savour.

WALKING INSTRUCTIONS - From the car park cross the footbridge over Helvellyn Gill to a stile. Bear right on the wide path to another footbridge and begin the ascent up[the zig-zag path with Helvellyn Gill on your left. Pass Browncove Crags and Lower Man with the ridge of White Side on your left. Ascend gently now to the summit of Helvellyn - you should be on the top within 2 hours from the car park! Descend to a cross shaped stone wall shelter and turn right, heading south towards Nethermost Pike. In a few yards on your left is a plaque to the first plane that landed on Helvellyn on December 22nd 1926. In less than 1/2 mile bear right before Nethermost Pike, and continue descending with views of Thirlmere. Descend around Birk Side and past Comb Crags to a stile and forest. Descend to another and a track. Turn right and basically keep on this track, which is well stiled, for the next three miles back to Swirls car park.

ULLSWATER AND PLACE FELL (675m.) - 9 MILES

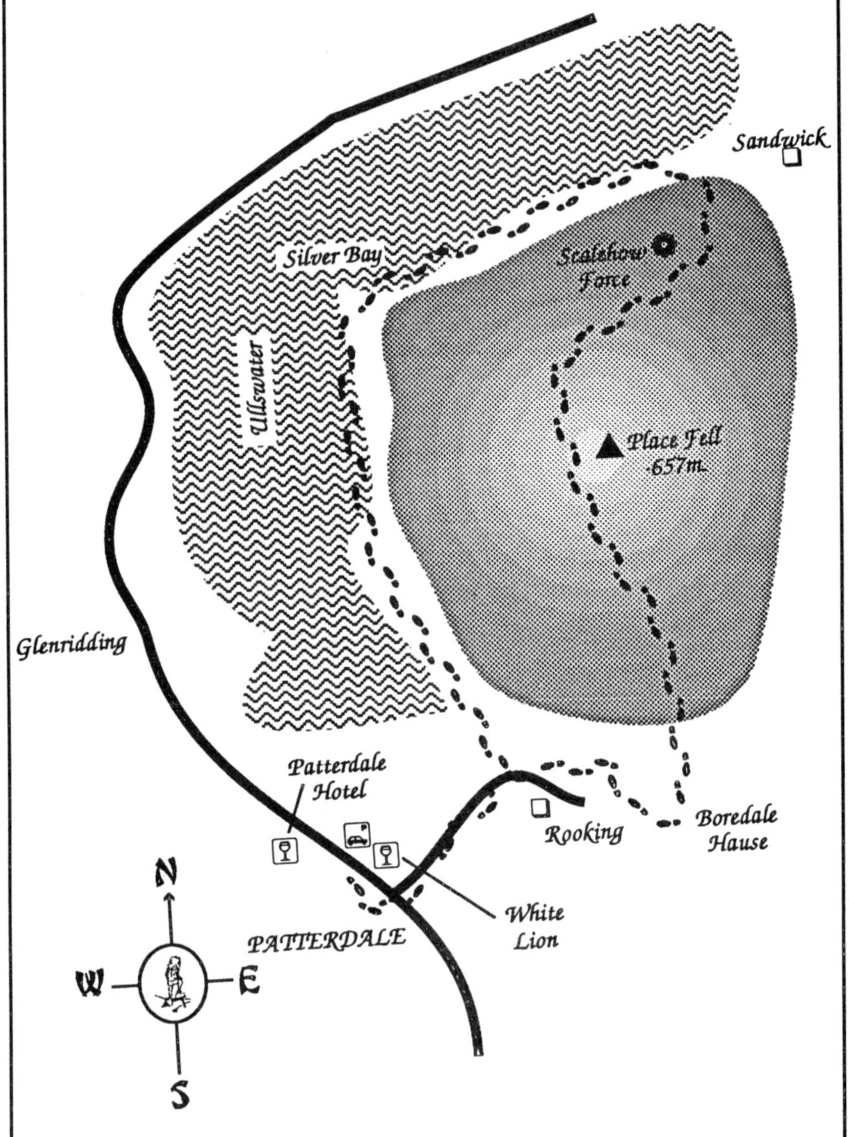

ULLSWATER AND PLACE FELL (657M.) - 9 MILES

- Allow 4 hours.

Patterdale - Ullswater - Silver Crag - Silver Bay - Scalehow Force - Place Fell - Boredale Hause - Patterdale.

1:25,000 Outdoor Leisure Map No. 5 - The English Lakes - North East Sheet.

Patterdale, near White Lion Inn.

Patterdale Hotel, White Lion Inn, Patterdale.

ABOUT THE WALK - Quite simply beautiful. The walk along the shore of Ullswater to Scalehow Force is exceptional and can be done as a shorter walk in its own right; even extending it to Sandwick. The crossing of the quiet and peaceful Place Fell is rewarding with extensive views over Ullswater and to the Helvellyn range. This is a magnificent walking area.

WALKING INSTRUCTIONS - From the car park return to the main road (A592) and turn left and left again soon afterwards, along the road towards Rooking. Follow it round to the houses and keep left on a track to a gate. Here is the bridlepath sign to *"Angle Tarn and Boredale Hause"* - your return route. Continue on the track and keep right where it forks. The track becomes a well defined gently ascending path and in little over a mile you pass Silver Crag on your left and descend towards Silver Bay. Here join the shore path and turn right along it. Keep on it for the next 1 1/2 miles to the footbridge near Scalehow Force. Cross and continue another 100 yards on the path/track. Here turn right and ascend the grass path which heads for the top lefthand side of the fall. Continue ascending path and in 1/2 mile pass a small quarry, In another 1/4 mile follow the path round to your right to a stone sheepfold. Follow the path to your left that ascends almost directly for the summit of Place Fell 1/2 mile away. Nearly 1/4 mile up here pass a water spring. From the summit head southwards, descending gently at first then more steeply to crossroads of paths at Boredale Hause. Here turn right and descend the bridlepath to Rooking, regaining your earlier route. Turn left and retrace your steps back to Patterdale.

Path to Silver Crag.

Shore path near Scalehow Force.

Approaching summit of Place Fell.

View to Glenridding.

HONISTER PASS AND HAY STACKS - 6 MILES

Erratic boulder.

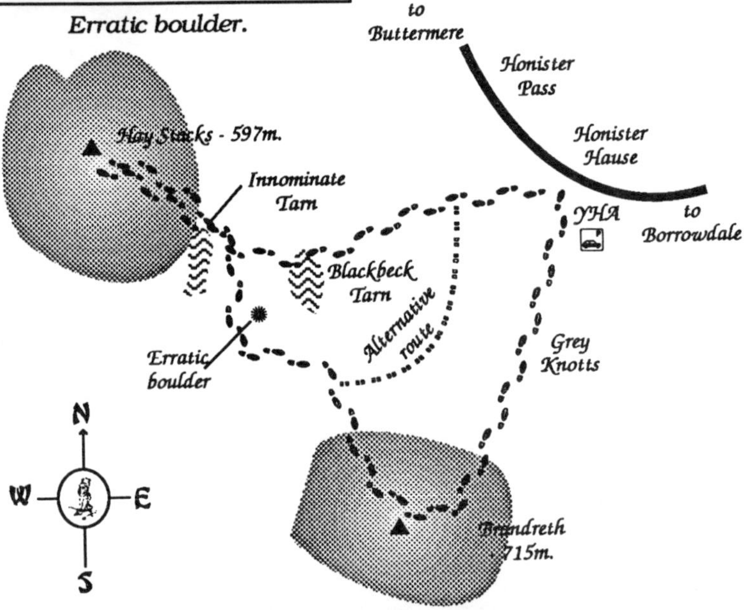

Blackbeck Tarn.

HONISTER PASS AND HAY STACKS - 6 MILES

- allow 2 1/2 hours.

Honister Pass - YHA - Drum House - Dubs Quarry - Blackbeck Tarn - Hay Stacks - Innominate Tarn - Erratic Boulder - Brandreth - Grey Knotts - Honister Pass.

1:25,000 Outdoor Leisure Map No. 4 - The English Lakes - North West Sheet.

- Honister Pass, beside Youth Hostel. Grid Ref. 225136.

- None.

ABOUT THE WALK - You start from the summit of Honister Pass and ascend gradually to old slate quarries before ascending to tarns and the summit of Haystack. Here are extensive views to Great and Green Gable. You cross broken ground to the summit of Brandreth before descending to Grey Knotts and back to Honister Pass. You can omit Brandreth and Grey Knotts, by following the cairned path back to you early path up the line of a dismantled tramway. A delightful walk with spectacular mountain views.

WALKING INSTRUCTIONS - From the car park at the Youth Hostel, return to the road and turn left and left again at the gate and footpath sign - *"Dubs"*. The path is well defined and basically follows the line of the dismantled Tramway. After 1/2 mile at *"Drum House"* you will see a path on your left; this is the lower path that can be used as your return missing out the summit of Brandreth and Grey Knotts. Continue on the line of the tramway to the disused Dubs Quarry. Walk through it and descend to a stream. Cross via stepping stones and ascend and in 1/2 mile pass Blackbeck Tarn on your left. On the far side you will see on the skyline an erratic boulder - you will walk past this later! Continue on the path past Innominate Tarn and onto the summit of Haystacks - 597m. Return to Innominate Tarn and just past it turn right. The path is a faint one but leads across broken ground to the right of the erratic boulder. Continue on the path and 1/4 mile from the boulder keep left and soon start gently ascending to the summit of Brandreth - 715m. Before it is a cairned path to your left which leads down to the former tramway, you passed earlier. Turn left and descend the broad ridge over Grey Knotts and down to Honister Pass, a mile from Brandreth's summit.

ENNERDALE WATER - 6 MILES

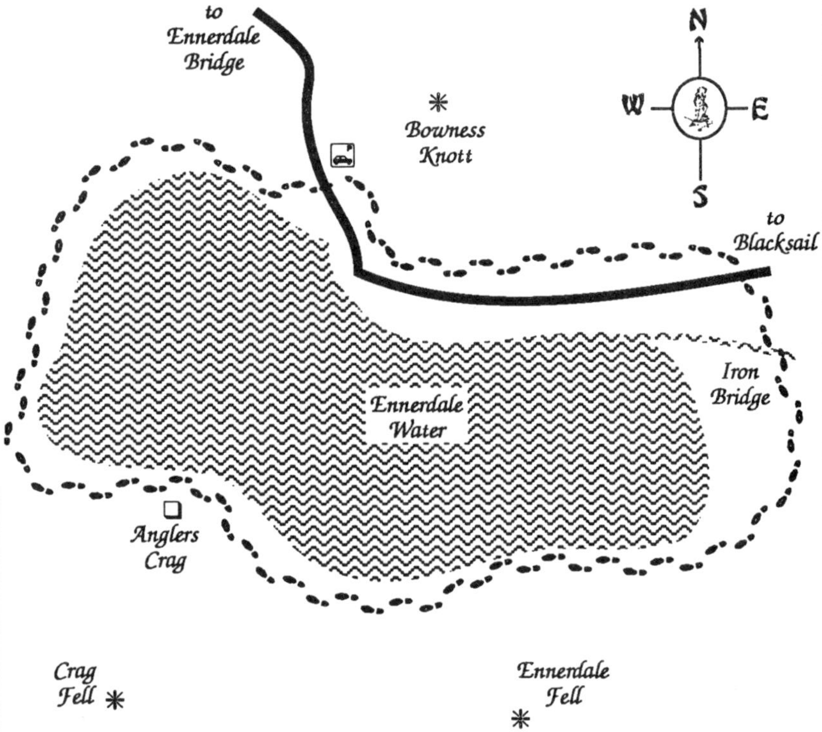

Newly shorn sheep heading back to the fells; Ennerdale Water on right.

ENNERDALE WATER - 6 MILES

- allow 2 1/2 hours.

- Ennerdale Forest car park - road - Iron Bridge - Shore Path - Anglers Crag - Shore path - Car Park.

1:25,000 Outdoor Leisure Map No. 4 - The English Lakes - North West Sheet.

- Near Bowness, Ennerdale. Grid Ref. 109154.

- None. Carry what you need - *"pack it in, pack it out."*

ABOUT THE WALK - Ennerdale, one of the remotest parts of the Lake District, has always been a favourite location of mine. The mountain scenery is spectacular and one of the finest Lakeland walks I have ever done is the Ennerdale horseshoe; mind you I am biased, it was a crystal clear day! The car park from the end of the road is a magnificent stepping off point for some great mountain days - to Pillar, Hay Stacks and Great Gable. If the weather is bad then the walk described here, around the shore of Ennerdale Water, makes a delightful change. The day I walked it the newly sheared sheep were being taken back onto the fells. The walk is done in an anti-clockwise direction.

WALKING INSTRUCTIONS - From the car park turn left along the road and basically keep on it for the next couple of miles. First above the water then you leave it behind and about 40 minutes from the car park is a path on your right down to an Iron Bridge over the River Liza. Cross this and continue up the field to a stile. Bear right and soon reach another. Keep the forest on your left and in 1/2 mile gain the shore of Ennerdale Water. For the remainder of the walk you follow a well defined path around the shore of the water. Well over 2 miles from the bridge walk around Anglers Crag and continue to the western end of the water. Using stiles continue around close to the shore and walk around the northern end before aiming for the car park. Near the car park leave the shore and bear left beside a wall to gain the road opposite the car park.

HOPEGILL HEAD - 770m - 5 MILES

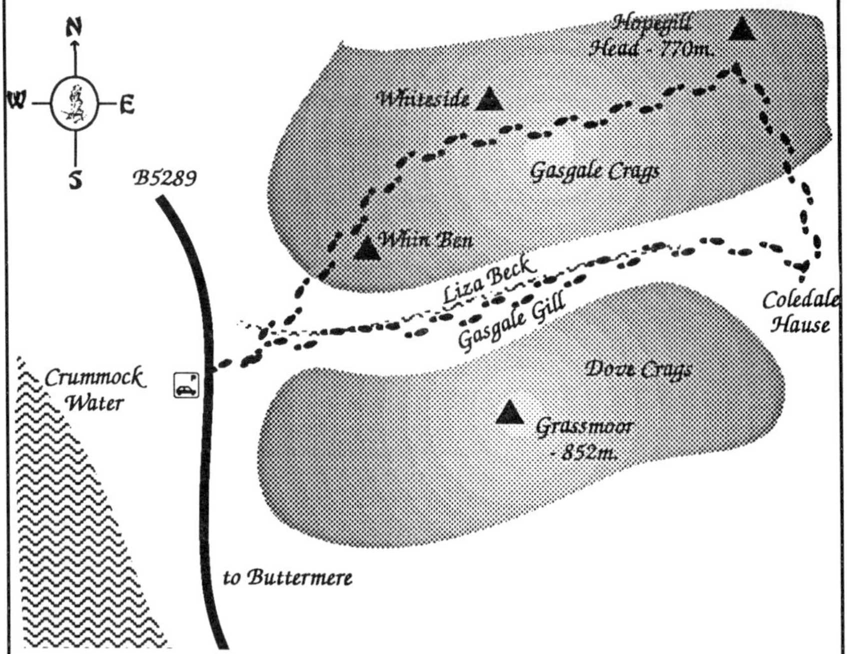

The ridge bewteen Hopegill Head and Whiteside.

HOPEGILL HEAD - 770m. - 5 MILES - allow 3 hours.

Lanthwaite - Liza Beck - Gasgale Gill - Coledale Hause - Sand Hill - Hopegill Head - Whiteside - Whin Ben - Llanthwaite.

O.S. MAP ***Map - 1:25,000 Outdoor Leisure map No. 4 - The English Lakes - North West Sheet.***

- Northern end of Crummock Water near Lanthwaite Green Farm. Grid Ref. 158207.

- None. Nearest at Buttermere.

ABOUT THE WALK - An exceptional high mountain walk. First you ascend Gasgale Gill to Coledale Hause, before ascending to the summit of Hopegill Head. From here you return along a spectacular ridge to Whiteside, before descending steeply back to Whin Ben and onto Lanthwaite. A short walk but a long ascent, with extensive mountain views.

WALKING INSTRUCTIONS - From the car park cross the road and follow the path across the grassland to Liza Beck and entrance to Gasgale Gill. Follow the path close to the beck and begin the gradual ascent, with the steep Gasgale Crags on your left, and Grasmoor and Dove Crags on your right. At the start of the beck, on your left is the hillock - Whin Ben - which is your return route. Follow the path for two miles; in the latter stages pass two waterfalls. Gaining the saddle at Coledale Hause, turn left and follow the well defined and cairned path to the summit of Hopegill Head, 770m. 1/2 mile away. Turn left and walk along the ridge of Whiteside, with Gasgale Crags below on your left. About a mile from Hopegill Head start descending steeply at first, and on towards Whin Ben. Continue descending back to your starting out path and retrace your steps back to Lanthwaite.

SPOUT FORCE & LORD'S SEAT - 2 1/2 and 4 1/2 MILES

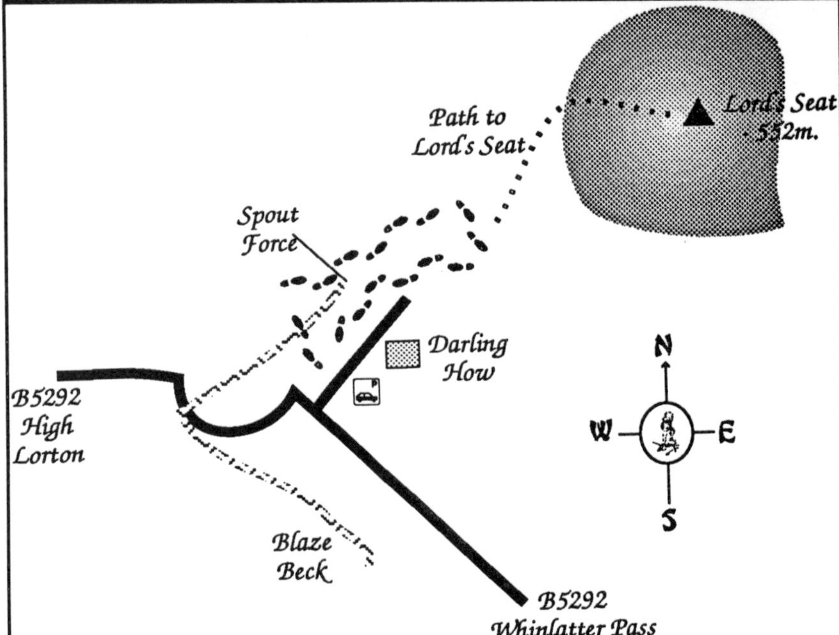

Spout Force and gorge.

SPOUT FORCE AND LORD'S SEAT - 2 1/2 & 4 1/2 MILES

- allow 1 to 2 hours.

Forestry Commission Car Park - Spout Force - Darling How Plantation - Lord's Seat - Darling How - Car Park.

O.S. MAP ***1:25,000 Outdoor Leisure Map No. 4 - The English Lakes - North West Sheet.***

P ***- Near Scawgill Bridge - Spout Force Car Park - Grid Ref. 182257.***

- None.

ABOUT THE WALK - A short walk following a Forestry Commission path to see the impressive waterfall, while encircling the area. The walk can be extended by ascending to the summit of Lord's Seat - 552m. - for views over Bassenthwaite Lake. While in the area a visit to the Whinlatter Forestry Visitor's Centre is well worthwhile.

WALKING INSTRUCTIONS - The Forestry Commission route is well stiled and marked by yellow banded square posts at regular intervals. From the small car park go through a stile and cross the field to the trees and descend to a footbridge over Blaze Beck. Turn right beside it and soon come to a viewpoint to Spout Force. Continue ascending on the path and cross a level area before more trees and onto a forest road bridge. Here turn right along the track to another and turn right. If you plan to ascend Lord's Seat, 1 1/2 miles away, turn left and follow the track and path beside the forest and on upto the summit; return the same way. Walk along the track a short distance before turning right along a signed path to Spout Force gorge , to reach a viewpoint opposite your earlier one. Follow the path round to your left back to the track and the farm - Darling How. Turn right along the track back to the car park.

ASHNESS BRIDGE & HIGH SEAT - 608m. - 3 or 6 MILES

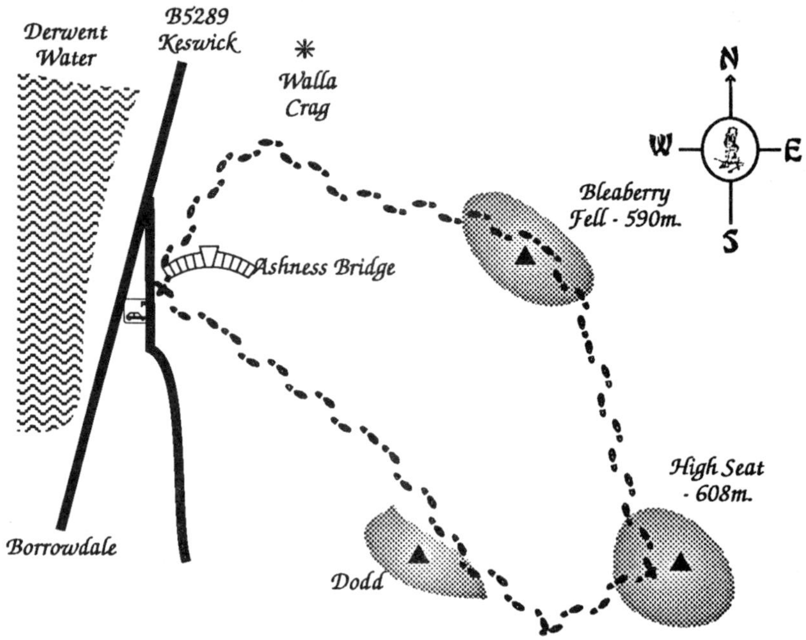

View to Derwent Water and Bassenthwaite Lake, from near Dodd Fell.

ASHNESS BRIDGE & HIGH SEAT - 608m. - 3 or 6 MILES

- allow 1 1/2 to 3 hours.

Ashness Bridge - Ashness Gull - High Seat - Bleaberry Fell - Ashness Bridge.

1:25,000 Outdoor Leisure map No. 4 - The English Lakes - North West Sheet.

Ashness Bridge. Grid Ref. 269196.

None

ABOUT THE WALK - On a clear summer's day, you will sit here and gaze at the stunning beauty of Derwent Water with Bassenthwaite Lake beyond. The scene of lakes and mountains is majestic. You can make this walk a short one to the summit of Dodd Fell (3 miles) or do the whole circuit (6 miles). Whatever you do, you have a most pleasant walk. The walk is done anti-clockwise and and involves approximately 600 metres of ascent.

WALKING INSTRUCTIONS - From the car park cross the road with Ashness Bridge well to your left, to a stile and footpath sign. Follow the well defined path beyond, gradually ascending Ashness Gill. After more than 1/2 mile pass a waterfall on your left. Just after to your right is a path to the summit of Dodd. Continue ahead near the gill and 1/2 mile from the waterfall bear left and ascend to the summit of High Seat - 608m., little over 1/4 mile away. Turn left at the summit, heading due north, for the summit of Bleaberry Fell - 590m. - approximately a mile away. From here the path bears left and descends towards the forest near Walla Crag, more than a mile away. After a mile you reach a path junction and turn left to continue descending back to Ashness Bridge.

Ashness Bridge.

WALK RECORD CHART

Date walked -

South Eastern area -

Grasmere and Rydal Water - 6 miles

Kentmere - 6 1/2 miles

Ambleside and Troutbeck - 8 miles

Hawshead and Latterbarrow - 6 miles

Grizedale Forest & Satterthwaite - 8 miles

South Western area -

Crinkle Crags & Pike of Blisco - 5 miles

Yewbarrow - 5 miles

Lligill Head & The Screes, Wast Water - 10 miles

North Eastern area -

Hellvellyn, 950m. - 8 miles

Ullswater and Place Fell - 9 miles

North Western area -

Honister Pass and Hay Stacks - 6 miles

Ennerdale Water - 6 miles

Hopegill Head - 770m, - 5 miles

Spout Force and Lord's Seat - 2 1/2 & 4 1/2 miles

Ashness Bridge & High Seat - 3 & 6 miles

THE JOHN MERRILL WALK BADGE

Complete six of the walks in this guide and get the above special John Merrill walk badge and signed certificate. Badges are black cloth with figure and lettering embroidered in four colours and measure 3 1/2" diameter.

BADGE ORDER FORM

Date and details of walks completed..

....

NAME ....

ADDRESS ....

....

Price: £2.75 each including postage, VAT and signed completion certificate.
Amount enclosed (Payable to Trail Crest Publications) ..
From: **TRAIL CREST PUBLICATIONS Ltd., Milne House, Speedwell Mill, Millers Green, Wirksworth, Derbyshire. DE4 4BL**
© /**Fax** (0629) 826354 - 24hr answering service.

************* YOU MAY PHOTOCOPY THIS FORM *********

"I'VE DONE A JOHN MERRILL WALK" T SHIRT -
Emerald Green with white lettering and walking man logo. Send £7.50 to Trail Crest Publications stating size required.

John Merrill's "Happy Walking!" Cap - £2.50

OBSERVE THE MOUNTAIN CODE

1. Plan, with maps.

2. Don't try too much too soon. Move gradually to bigger things.

3. Go with others and keep together always. Until experienced don't take charge of others: then take only ten or less.

4. Equip against the worst. Be well shod: have warm clothing and a waterproof cover, spare clothes and food for all, map, whistle, torch and compass.

5. Give yourself ample time, and more as a reserve. Move steadily. Don't hurry and don't waste time.

6. Don't throw down or dislodge rocks or stones. Know and observe the Country Code.

7. Eye the weather it can change completely in a few hours. Don't go on recklessly if it turns bad. Don't be afraid to come down.

8. Don't go rock, snow or ice climbing without an experienced leader.

9. If lost don't panic or rush down. Keep together and deliberately work out your position and your best way down.

10. Leave word behind you of your route and when you expect to be back. If you arrive where friends don't expect you, 'phone them or tell the police (to save needless searches).

WIN A RUCKSACK!

- 35 litre day pack.

- value £30.

All the walks in this book were walked over 5 1/2 days. The first person to write in with the correct order they were done in will get a free rucksack. The next five successful entrants will receive some small "goodies" and a £1.00 John Merrill book voucher. Offer closes - 31st. December 1993.

Send you entry to -

John Merrill
Lakeland Competition,
Trail Crest Publications Ltd.,
Milne House,
Speedwell Mill,
Millers Green,
Wirksworth,
Derbyshire.
DE4 4BL.

"from footprint to finished book"

OTHER BOOKS by John N. Merrill Published by TRAIL CREST PUBLICATIONS Ltd.

CIRCULAR WALK GUIDES -

SHORT CIRCULAR WALKS IN THE PEAK DISTRICT - Vol. 1 and 2
CIRCULAR WALKS IN WESTERN PEAKLAND
SHORT CIRCULAR WALKS IN THE STAFFORDSHIRE MOORLANDS
SHORT CIRCULAR WALKS - TOWNS & VILLAGES OF THE PEAK DISTRICT
SHORT CIRCULAR WALKS AROUND MATLOCK
SHORT CIRCULAR WALKS IN THE DUKERIES
SHORT CIRCULAR WALKS IN SOUTH YORKSHIRE
SHORT CIRCULAR WALKS IN SOUTH DERBYSHIRE
SHORT CIRCULAR WALKS AROUND BUXTON
SHORT CIRCULAR WALKS AROUND WIRKSWORTH
SHORT CIRCULAR WALKS IN THE HOPE VALLEY
40 SHORT CIRCULAR WALKS IN THE PEAK DISTRICT
CIRCULAR WALKS ON KINDER & BLEAKLOW
SHORT CIRCULAR WALKS IN SOUTH NOTTINGHAMSHIRE
SHIRT CIRCULAR WALKS IN CHESHIRE
SHORT CIRCULAR WALKS IN WEST YORKSHIRE
CIRCULAR WALKS TO PEAK DISTRICT AIRCRAFT WRECKS by John Mason
CIRCULAR WALKS IN THE DERBYSHIRE DALES
SHORT CIRCULAR WALKS IN EAST DEVON
SHORT CIRCULAR WALKS AROUND HARROGATE
SHORT CIRCULAR WALKS IN CHARNWOOD FOREST
SHORT CIRCULAR WALKS AROUND CHESTERFIELD
SHORT CIRCULAR WALKS IN THE YORKS DALES - Vol 1 - Southern area.
SHORT CIRCULAR WALKS IN THE AMBER VALLEY (Derbyshire)
SHORT CIRCULAR WALKS IN THE LAKE DISTRICT
SHORT CIRCULAR WALKS IN EAST STAFFORDSHIRE
LONG CIRCULAR WALKS IN THE PEAK DISTRICT - Vol.1 and 2.
LONG CIRCULAR WALKS IN THE STAFFORDSHIRE MOORLANDS
LONG CIRCULAR WALKS IN CHESHIRE
WALKING THE TISSINGTON TRAIL
WALKING THE HIGH PEAK TRAIL

CANAL WALKS -

VOL 1 - DERBYSHIRE & NOTTINGHAMSHIRE
VOL 2 - CHESHIRE & STAFFORDSHIRE
VOL 3 - STAFFORDSHIRE
VOL 4 - THE CHESHIRE RING
VOL 5 - LINCOLNSHIRE & NOTTINGHAMSHIRE
VOL 6 - SOUTH YORKSHIRE
VOL 7 - THE TRENT & MERSEY CANAL

JOHN MERRILL DAY CHALLENGE WALKS -

WHITE PEAK CHALLENGE WALK
DARK PEAK CHALLENGE WALK
PEAK DISTRICT END TO END WALKS
STAFFORDSHIRE MOORLANDS CHALLENGE WALK
THE LITTLE JOHN CHALLENGE WALK

YORKSHIRE DALES CHALLENGE WALK
NORTH YORKSHIRE MOORS CHALLENGE WALK
LAKELAND CHALLENGE WALK
THE RUTLAND WATER CHALLENGE WALK
MALVERN HILLS CHALLENGE WALK
THE SALTER'S WAY
THE SNOWDON CHALLENGE
CHARNWOOD FOREST CHALLENGE WALK
THREE COUNTIES CHALLENGE WALK (Peak District).

INSTRUCTION & RECORD -
HIKE TO BE FIT.....STROLLING WITH JOHN
THE JOHN MERRILL WALK RECORD BOOK

MULTIPLE DAY WALKS -
THE RIVERS'S WAY
PEAK DISTRICT: HIGH LEVEL ROUTE
PEAK DISTRICT MARATHONS
THE LIMEY WAY
THE PEAKLAND WAY

COAST WALKS & NATIONAL TRAILS -
ISLE OF WIGHT COAST PATH
PEMBROKESHIRE COAST PATH
THE CLEVELAND WAY
WALKING ANGELSEY'S COASTLINE.

PEAK DISTRICT HISTORICAL GUIDES -
A to Z GUIDE OF THE PEAK DISTRICT
DERBYSHIRE INNS - an A to Z guide
HALLS AND CASTLES OF THE PEAK DISTRICT & DERBYSHIRE
TOURING THE PEAK DISTRICT & DERBYSHIRE BY CAR
DERBYSHIRE FOLKLORE
PUNISHMENT IN DERBYSHIRE
CUSTOMS OF THE PEAK DISTRICT & DERBYSHIRE
WINSTER - a souvenir guide
ARKWRIGHT OF CROMFORD
LEGENDS OF DERBYSHIRE
DERBYSHIRE FACTS & RECORDS
TALES FROM THE MINES by Geoffrey Carr
PEAK DISTRICT PLACE NAMES by Martin Spray

JOHN MERRILL'S MAJOR WALKS -
TURN RIGHT AT LAND'S END
WITH MUSTARD ON MY BACK
TURN RIGHT AT DEATH VALLEY
EMERALD COAST WALK

SKETCH BOOKS -
SKETCHES OF THE PEAK DISTRICT

COLOUR BOOK:-
THE PEAK DISTRICT.......something to remember her by.

OVERSEAS GUIDES -
HIKING IN NEW MEXICO - Vol I - The Sandia and Manzano Mountains.
Vol 2 - Hiking "Billy the Kid" Country.
"WALKING IN DRACULA COUNTRY" - Romania.